Wait On God

What Every Single Woman Should Know to Receive God's Best!

Briana G. Whitaker

ISBN-10: 1937660435
ISBN-13: 978-1-937660-43-7
eBook ISBN-13: 978-1-937660-48-2
Library of Congress Control Number: 2014958879

Published by:

 HERITAGE PRESS
PUBLICATIONS

Heritage Press Publications, LLC
PO Box 561
Collinsville, MS 39325

Editors: Nikki Hill and Hanne E. Moon
Book and cover design: Lisa Thomson, BZ Studio

Dedication

This book is dedicated to all my single sisters in Christ who desire to please God in their relationships and do things His way. "Seek ye first the kingdom of God, and His righteousness; and all these things will be added unto you" (Matthew 6:33 KJV). I'm a living witness that waiting on God pays off. Be blessed with God's best!

I also dedicate this book to my grandmother, the late Mrs. Ruth Rhodes Lancaster, who I miss dearly. I wish that you could share in this moment with me, but I know that you will always be with me from your Heavenly home and in my heart. I will always love you.

"Wait on the Lord; be of good courage, and he shall strengthen thine heart: wait, I say, on the Lord."
(Psalms 37:14 KJV)

"But they that wait upon the Lord shall renew their strength; they shall mount up with wings as eagles; they shall run, and not be weary; and they shall walk, and not faint."
(Isaiah 40:31 KJV)

Table of Contents

Foreword

Some people carve a place in your heart that will remain for a lifetime. This is the kind of impression that Briana has made in our lives since we met her in 1998. Beginning as a shy and somewhat unsure young lady, we have had the pleasure of watching her mature into a wise, bold, and strong woman of God. Her impact upon the ministry with her love for the Lord, diligence in His work, and commitment to her relationship with Him are undeniable.

Through her example, she has encouraged many young women to wait on the Lord and receive the fullness of the blessings He has in store for them. We have seen Briana as a single woman and as a wife. We can truly say that she has carried each title with equal grace.

We have watched her walk with God throughout the years. By standing firmly on the Word of God, Briana is a true example of what it means to wait on God. In writing this book, she is not just sharing wisdom, but her testimony of how patiently following God's path leads to the blessings that God has set aside for each of us.

Pastor Stanley E. Hayes, Sr. and Elect Lady Julie A. Hayes

Acknowledgements

I'd like to give honor where honor is due by acknowledging some key people who have made writing this book possible.

First, I want to give all praises to my Lord and Savior Jesus Christ who has gifted me with many gifts and talents, but especially the gift to bless the body of Christ through the written word. I could not have done it without His Word, His inspiration, and His grace.

I would also like to give double honor to my Ministry Gift, Pastor Stanley E. Hayes, Sr. and Elect Lady Julie Ann Hayes of the Enon Missionary Baptist Church in Sumter, South Carolina. Every insight that I have shared in this book came by the revelation that I have received under your teaching and leadership. Thank you for ministering the unadulterated Word of God with such boldness, conviction, and clarity. Truly I could never repay you for the spiritual wisdom that you have sown into my life. I pray that God uses this unique opportunity that He has given me to be a blessing to you two in return.

I give honor to my loving husband, Russell Whitaker, Jr., my muse. You are God's manifested promise in my life, and I consider you the BEST He could have offered to me. Thank you for loving me unconditionally, listening to me continually, and lending me your support in every way imaginable. You still make my heart dance because you are the best husband ever! I love you. Thank you to my mother-in-love, Mrs. Mary L. King, for raising your son to be a man of God and for instilling God's Word in him at a young age. I love you too!

I also honor my mom, Ms. Carrie M. Lancaster, for her constant love and support my entire life. Mom, I am the woman of God I am today because of you. I am crying as I write this because when the odds were against you, you stood strong and raised me as a single mother, and you did so with such grace and skill. I am grateful to have such a strong, dependable, and godly mother in you.

And lastly, I want to acknowledge my sisters in Christ, the virtuous ladies of the Young Women in Action Ministry (YWA) of Enon Missionary Baptist Church. Thank you for allowing me to be your leader for all of these years. I also thank you for holding me accountable to the Word of God, by praying for me, and for encouraging me. It is a privilege to serve in ministry alongside you, and I pray that you are all blessed with God's best in every area of your lives.

The Promise Fulfilled

In April of 2011, at the age of thirty, I married the man of my dreams. After all the years of waiting and wishing, hoping and praying, God sent my prince. And what's ironic about our love story is that during all the years of waiting and wishing, hoping and praying, he (my husband) had been there all along. I was just too blind to see it. For years we had shared a church. We had heard the same sermons and shared the same beliefs, but we were totally oblivious to the possibility of being with each other. All the time I wondered, *Where is my future husband and when will we meet?* Yeah, sure, I dated "unsuccessfully" for quite some time, not even realizing the blessing that was right under my nose, or more appropriately, a few pews over, waiting to be revealed by God and acknowledged by me.

I worried that God, with His sense of humor, would send me someone whom I would least expect as my mate. "Please Lord, don't let it be someone I'm not attracted to," I would beg. I wanted him to be good-looking, saved, and a member of my church—a BMW—Black Man Worshiping. Well, I got all that and more in my husband, Russell.

What I've learned from my experience is that I was so obsessed with the idea of being married that I became blind to reality. Blindness here is not just the inability to see, it's the inability to see clearly and with sound judgment, as one should. Let me explain.

Sometimes, when looking too hard for anything, one never sees it staring them right in the face—right where it should be or where it was left. I recently misplaced my digital camera battery charger. I searched and searched everywhere I thought it would be, but to no avail. Finally, I decided to just buy another one to replace it since I would need my camera in the near future. I quickly changed my mind though when I found out how much a replacement would cost. Not wanting to spend the money myself, I asked my husband to buy it for me as a Christmas gift.

A few days before Christmas, I decided to tidy up my room a bit. I threw away junk mail and all sorts of other clutter invading my space. After about an hour of this, I discovered my battery charger right where I had left it and where I had looked for it weeks before. I couldn't find it then for two reasons: first, it was hidden by piles of junk and second, I was focusing too hard on it. It wasn't until I straightened up a few things and forgot about my hunt for it that it presented itself to me. The same is true in the case of my husband. Like the battery charger, he was right before my eyes, right where God put Him and where I believed he would be, but he was concealed by both *my* superficial expectations and *my* obsession to find him. Yes, ladies, I said "find him," which was my mistake. The Bible says in Proverbs 18:22 (NIV) that, "Whoso findeth a wife findeth a good thing." I wasn't supposed to be searching in the first place! And then there was my lengthy list of desirable qualities.

The laundry list went on and on: he should be this complexion, have this job, make this amount of money, stand this tall, and be this age. Not to forget, he must be saved and share my same beliefs concerning spiritual matters. Over the years, however, the former list began to dwindle and the latter became paramount. It became more important to me that my husband possess certain spiritual qualities like patience, generosity, kindness, gentleness, faith, and love. If he had all these things, then quite naturally all the rest of the physical attributes would follow. And they did. While my husband doesn't earn a six-figure salary or drive a fancy car, he makes me very happy, and we complement each other quite well both physically and spiritually.

Now, you may also be at a place in your life where you desire to be married and are wondering, perhaps a little more often than you'd like, when you will meet your mate or when you will marry the one you're dating now. Fear of the unknown may be causing you to be anxious, and you may be tempted to step ahead of God in the process. But hold on, my sister! Don't give up! This book is for you.

The Bible clearly states that God is no respecter of persons, which means that what He's done for me, He can and will do for you. I want to challenge you to take a step of faith and wait for your mate. This book contains the nine key strategies that I have learned along the way that may help you WAIT ON GOD.

One last note: at the end of each chapter, you will find a section titled "The Waiting Room." This is a section for the ideas I've presented in that chapter. There are questions and writing prompts designed to help you self-reflect and confessions designed to help build your faith in each area. Here you are safe to explore, ponder, brainstorm, express your thoughts, and encourage yourself in the Lord with no limitations. Don't worry about right or wrong—just be honest with yourself and let God direct you as He chooses! Happy waiting!

Briana G. Whitaker

CHAPTER 1

Wish Others Well

"Knowing that whatsoever good thing any man doeth, the same shall he receive of the Lord, whether he be bond or free."
(Ephesians 6:8 KJV)

Have you ever heard the saying, "always a bridesmaid and never a bride?" To me, it's such a pessimistic statement that suggests one will always be in that state and that everyone deserves to be happy but you. If you find yourself feeling that way, make sure that, before you accept another bridesmaid invitation, you get your heart in the right place. We don't want to sabotage someone else's special day with a sour attitude, do we?

Truth is, it's easy to find yourself envying another couple, especially when your relationships don't seem to be heading in the right direction. In spite of how you may be feeling, this is the time to wish them well all the more. Here's why: jealousy is the devil's tool to get you off course for your blessing. Let's consider the example of Cain and Abel, the most famous story of jealousy found in the Bible.

Cain and Abel both brought offerings to God, but Abel's first-fruit offering was accepted by God, and Cain's was not. Cain, feeling rejected, became very angry, and that anger quickly turned to jealousy. *What does Abel have that I don't?* he must have thought to himself, and God answered the question for him. I can imagine Him saying, "Cain, step your game up. Your brother did well in bringing me the first and best of his flock. You, on the other hand, did not do well because you brought me what you thought I should have." After hearing from God, Cain still harbored resentment toward his brother. But what Cain didn't realize was that Abel, a flesh and blood being, was not his enemy. His enemy was sin, crouching at his door, desiring to have him. Unfortunately, he gave himself over to the sin rather than taking control of it. The product of his jealous rage? A dead baby brother. The result of his cold-blooded murder? Banishment from the very presence of God. On top of that, he forfeited all God had to offer him and received a lifestyle as a fugitive and vagabond for the rest of his days on earth. Was it worth it? Obviously not, as spiritual death is far worse than physical death. If only he had channeled those negative emotions into a more positive direction (like finding out how he could get his offering accepted the next time), Cain would have remained in his place of blessing.

Truth is, it's easy to find yourself envying another couple, especially when your relationships don't seem to be heading in the right direction. In spite of how you may be feeling, this is the time to wish them well all the more. Here's why: jealousy is the devil's tool to get you off course for your blessing.

I, too, was tempted in this area. I had several friends who married before me, and while I love them and was very happy for them, the sin of jealousy did crouch at my door to see how I would handle it. What did I do? I attended the weddings, participated in the weddings, gave gifts at the weddings, and took the pictures at the weddings—everything the devil didn't want me to do. Unlike Cain, I took control of the emotion instead of letting it control me.

But the bigger challenge is being happy for those whom you know haven't honored God in their dating relationships and still end up with the fairy tale wedding. Let me insert this point right here, ladies. Situations like this will definitely be a problem for you if you see getting married as "the prize," when actually, it's not. A man isn't the prize—God is. He is our exceedingly great reward, and marriage is just an extension of our relationship with Him. Before I got this revelation though, I remember being devastated one night after finding out that a friend of mine was soon to be married AND that she had a baby on the way. I was angry, not so much because she was getting married, but because of the circumstances surrounding the marriage. In no way am I anyone's judge. I just knew some of the things that went on in the relationship, and it was not an ideal situation according to God's divine order. I was suffering from the fretting syndrome that David talks about in Psalm 37 (NIV).

> *Do not fret because of those who are evil*
> > *or be envious of those who do wrong. (verse 1a)*

> *Be still before the Lord*
> > *and wait patiently for him;*
> *do not fret when people succeed in their ways,*
> > *when they carry out their wicked schemes. (verse 7)*

Here I was, a twenty-eight-year-old virgin, trying desperately to keep myself for my husband—the one that God had promised for honoring His Word. Why was it that I couldn't seem to find the love I so deserved when others who were obviously NOT doing things God's way were getting all the play and the husbands too? To me, it just wasn't fair! Like Cain, I thought, *What does she have that I don't?* That night, I cried myself to sleep, pleading my case before God. I probably sounded really pathetic to Him. I sensed this as I woke up the next morning, and I felt guilty for not seeing the good in the situation and being genuinely happy for my friend the night before. I soon got myself together and prepared to attend a beautiful wedding with a smile on my face and joy in my heart for their union.

What Every Single Woman Should Know to Receive God's Best!

A man isn't the prize—God is. He is our exceedingly great reward and marriage is just an extension of our relationship with Him.

So how do we combat the vicious spirit of jealousy? I think we need to understand and settle some things once and for all. First, the devil wants believers to fret. He's like the busybody in school who always instigates fights and stirs up confusion. He starts it, but when it's time to confront the offender, he leaves you high and dry and looking mighty foolish. Those are opportunities he uses to gain a foothold in our lives. With that foothold, he tries to run things, but I have decided not to give him the opportunity any longer, and so should you.

Next, know what is actually happening when we fret ourselves. When we fret, we blaze up with anger and jealousy about a situation over which we have no control. Can you say waste of time and energy? David warned against fretting about the ungodly actions and decisions of others that seem to lead to favorable consequences for them. That is not your concern. It's God's. Your only concern should be God's promises to you because He's faithful to perform them, and the Bible reminds us of this repeatedly!

1. "...but those that wait upon the Lord, they shall inherit the earth." (Psalms 37:9b KJV)

2. "Delight thyself also in the Lord; and he shall give thee the desires of thine heart." (Psalms 37:4 KJV)

3. "Commit thy way unto the Lord; trust also in him; and he shall bring it to pass." (Psalms 37:5 KJV)

4. "But seek ye first the kingdom of God, and his righteousness; and all these things shall be added unto you." (Matthew 6:33 KJV)

When we keep our focus on our own relationship with the Father, we avoid the trap of jealousy and enjoy an abundance of peace (Psalms 37:11b KJV).

Lastly, when you feel a twinge of jealousy creeping down your neck, say and do the opposite of what you are feeling. That's where your victory lies. Like the Bible says in Revelation 12:11 (KJV), "You overcome by the word of your testimony." So say something kind, encourage them, heck, buy them a gift (that'll really whup the devil's butt!). You'll find that celebrating another couple's success and genuinely being concerned for their well-being will actually do you some good. Being jealous of other relationships only makes you bitter and unable to see the good that is already in your life. I've learned that the good things I make happen for others, God will make happen for me. In other words, my prayer for other couples will yield others praying for my relationship. My rejoicing for other couples in happy moments will yield others rejoicing over my relationship successes. Get it?

Bottom line—no matter how it's accessorized or what the occasion, jealousy is not an outfit you want to be caught dead in. It only detracts from your God-given beauty.

The Waiting Room

1. Have you ever been jealous of someone else's relationship?

   _____

   _____

2. How did the jealousy affect the way you treated them or behaved around them?

   _____

   _____

3. In what ways will you combat jealousy of others in relationships?

   _____

   _____

4. What would you do differently now that you know jealousy's harmful effect on you receiving God's best for you?

   _____

   _____

 Say this in faith...

I am a believer and not a doubter. I walk by faith and not by sight (2 Corinthians 5:7). I am full of joy and peace. The love of God is shed abroad in my heart by the Holy Ghost (Romans 5:5). I love everybody, and I rejoice with those who rejoice and weep for those who weep. Jealousy has no place in me. I resist the spirit of jealousy. I am blessed to be a blessing to others. I wish others well, and I am genuinely happy when others are blessed. God is not a respecter of persons (Acts 10:34). What He does for one, He will do also for me. I take advantage of every opportunity I have to do good to others and because of that, God sees to it that good is done for me. I do not fret because of evildoers (Psalms 37:7). I wait patiently on the Lord to bring His promises concerning me to pass. In Jesus's name.

Reflection—what does it all mean to you?

_____

_____

_____

_____

_____

_____

_____

CHAPTER 2

Abstain from Fleshly Lusts

"Dearly beloved, I beseech you as strangers and pilgrims, abstain from fleshly lusts, which war against the soul." (1 Peter 2:11 KJV)

"For this is the will of God, even your sanctification, that ye should abstain from fornication."
(1 Thessalonians 4:3 KJV)

Newsflash! As born-again believers, our bodies are not our own to do whatever we want, whenever we want. Quite the contrary, in fact. The body is for God and God for the body. It is to be used to glorify Him, not to please ourselves through premarital sex. In other words, abstinence is God's will for you, my single sister.

Although it is a challenge to remain sexually pure these days, it is for your benefit. When fornication is introduced into your relationship, it brings all sorts of unnecessary problems with it, and it clouds your judgment, keeping you from making godly decisions. You will thank God you waited for your wedding night to experience the joys of intercourse, as He promises in His Word to bless those who keep His Word. I know we did.

About four months into my dating relationship with my husband, I was asked to sit on a church panel for a women's seminar on healthy marriages and relationships. Serving on the panel were my pastor's wife, a woman married for more than forty years, a woman married for twenty years, a newlywed, and me—a young, single woman. Everyone shared their various experiences with dating and marriage. When it was my turn, I talked about the importance of establishing boundaries and not putting ourselves in compromising situations. For example, if you know that by midnight you are feeling sleepy and a little less guarded, then it is probably not a good idea to be alone with your sweetie at that time. Establish the boundary to end the night at an earlier hour. And if you know that hot and heavy kissing gets you more excited than you should be, it is probably not a good idea to do it. Ladies, I am not trying to spoil your fun. I am only trying to get you to make smarter decisions about your dating interactions. Besides, it is for your protection.

And let's face it—we are all human with natural human feelings and desires. Those things are nothing to play with, and God knows it too, which is why He said this:

"It is good for a man not to touch a woman. Nevertheless, to avoid fornication, let every man have his own wife, and let every woman have her own husband." (1 Corinthians 7:2 KJV)

What may seem like harmless petting soon turns into a fleshly lust—a bodily longing for what is forbidden and, as children of God, it is from these that we are warned to abstain for good reason. We all know that to every action there is a reaction, and when the actions are kissing mixed with touching, the reaction is not going to be anything you will be proud of in the morning.

Here's an analogy that may help put things in perspective. Relationships are like sports. Establishing physical boundaries in a relationship is like establishing boundaries in a game of basketball. When there are boundaries established, everybody knows what goes and what doesn't. There's no guessing and no grey area. What's out of bounds is out of bounds, which means that play is over. The other team gets possession of the ball. If there were no boundaries, there would be chaos, no control, and the rules would be impossible to follow. Similarly, failing to establish boundaries in a relationship makes it difficult for you to follow God's command to abstain from fornication, which puts you in an unprotected place—out of His will. It also puts you in a position to be out of control and unable to think rationally. These lusts war against your very soul. The real you (your spirit) can know the right thing to do, but, because your flesh appetite has been fulfilled, it won't stop fighting your spirit until it gets more of what it desires. More importantly, it gives Satan, your enemy, possession of your peace and the promises God intends for you.

Establishing boundaries in a relationship makes both people aware of what goes and what doesn't. It allows you to follow God's command to abstain from fornication, which puts you in a place of protection—in His will. It also helps you remain in control and able to think rationally, and it puts you, not Satan, in possession of your peace and the promises God intends for you.

I was determined not to be subject to Satan, and I wanted to be a good example for others. So, at the seminar, I decided to share my little secret about being a virgin. I was a little hesitant because I didn't want to come off as pompous. Quite the contrary, I wanted everyone to know that not everyone was sexually active, and that it was possible to be kept in today's society. Not only did I share my status, but I also declared in front of about one hundred women and girls from my church that I would remain in that state until I got married. While it was liberating, I knew that my declaration would cause my flesh to rebel, and it did try. But despite the challenges to my faith, I accomplished my goal to marry as a virgin, and I wouldn't change a thing about that.

Now that I am married, I can admit that sex is good and good for you, if done in the right context. I'd like to debunk one myth that I heard from a friend of mine while I was dating Russell: try out the man sexually before marriage. Ladies, dating is not shoe shopping. When I shop for shoes, I

Similarly, failing to establish boundaries in a relationship makes it difficult for you to follow God's command to abstain from fornication, which puts you in an unprotected place—out of His will.

find all the shoes that are cute, on sale, and in my size (though I have gone a shoe size down because a shoe was super cute). On top of that, I don't even stop at one store! That's a lot of shoes in one shopping trip.

But is that how we as female believers should treat the men we date? Does it make sense to "try out" every man I find attractive until I find the right one? Absolutely NOT!

But some would argue that you don't want to marry and not be sexually fulfilled. Well, I ask, is there anything too hard for God? Do you really think He was wrong in commanding that we abstain from fornication? He knew the risks both physically and spiritually with indulging prematurely.

This reminds me of an analogy I heard a while ago by Bishop T.D. Jakes. He compared fornication to a child with a razor. Shaving is a task in which adult men partake to make themselves look presentable. It's perfectly acceptable and in some ways, a rite of passage into manhood. An adult male knows how to handle a razor with care. However, put that same razor into the hands of a child, and you've got the potential for disaster. Why? Because the child is not equipped to handle the responsibility of shaving, just like a single Christian is not equipped to handle the responsibility of sex before marriage. Yes, you have the right physical equipment to make it happen, but the most important equipment (like God's blessing and protection, emotional security, commitment, and spiritual peace) is missing if you're single. If playing with razors can get you cut, playing with sex outside of marriage can earn you unnecessary spiritual, emotional, and physical scarring.

Remember, everything good is not always good for you if done at the wrong time and under the wrong conditions—namely out of the will of God. Sex is good because God made it, but sex before marriage is deadly. Deadly? That's a bit extreme, you might be saying. Well, physical death is not the only death that exists. We all know that there are cases where physical death is a consequence of irresponsible sexual activity. What about the effect to your spiritual life? I am talking to born-again believers who live by the Word, right? Fornication is sin, and sin separates us from God.

And what about the effect on your mind? You just can't argue with the Word! It clearly states that, "Thou wilt keep him in perfect peace, whose mind is stayed on thee (Isaiah 26:3 KJV)." It's hard to keep your mind on God when you are battling with the flesh that wants what it wants when it wants it. The flesh is already a mess as it is, but add to it the false pleasure of sexual sin, and you've really got a hot mess. How can your mind be at peace in a war of lust? It can't. However, doing things God's way does give you peace, and God's way is abstinence. Going into a marriage without yet knowing your partner intimately minimizes the amount of baggage being brought into the relationship and maximizes trust and peace in the home.

While single, I learned another important lesson about the dangers of lust. James 1:14-15 (KJV) says, "But every man is tempted, when he is drawn away of his own lust, and enticed. Then when lust hath conceived, it bringeth forth sin: and sin, when it is finished, bringeth forth death." The word *lust* in this verse is defined as a longing or desire. Like so many women, what I had was a desire to be married—a strong one. Well, marriages are ordained by God, and He said that He would give me the desires of my heart, right? Exactly, but God does not want your harmless and very acceptable desire to go haywire. That's exactly what a lust is, and that is what Satan wants—to take something so normal and natural, such as a desire to be married, and pervert it. If you're not careful, he will have you lusting after things and people who are forbidden. He will have you constantly on the lookout for your next encounter with "the one." He will have you thinking that every attractive man that walks through the door could be your husband. And if you give in to this lust, you'll become consumed with the thought of it. You'll refuse to go anywhere without looking like you stepped off of the runway.

Ladies, this is no way to live freely, and the danger is that it is a sign you no longer trust God to bring your husband into your life. If you're not trusting God, then you're not in faith, and anything that is not of faith is sin, which separates us from God. James goes on to say in verse sixteen and seventeen, "Do not err, my beloved brethren. Every good gift and every perfect gift is from above, and cometh down from the Father of lights, with whom is no variableness, neither shadow of turning" (KJV). So I say to you, do not be deceived, my dear sisters. God is the only one who can give you what is perfect for you. GOD. Not the devil. Not even you.

Please understand, I don't say any of these things about abstinence to be judgmental or high minded. I know the struggle is real! Satan wouldn't be able to deceive so many people if it weren't. I only say this as someone who has lived it and, by the grace of God, done it His way. If you haven't already crossed that line in your relationship, please heed these words and do not until the time is right—when you and your mate enter a marriage covenant. If you have crossed that line in your relationship, thank God for His grace, redemptive power, and forgiveness, and vow to present your body as a living sacrifice to God from here on out (Romans 12:2). You don't have to do it alone. The Holy Spirit is ever ready and willing to help.

I honestly believe that my marriage would not be as successful as it is now if we had indulged in sex prematurely. The guilt of disappointing the people who looked up to me would have eaten me alive, which brings up another important point—accountability. You will have much greater success with abstinence if you are accountable to someone. For me, it was all the ladies at my church who heard my testimony. For you, it might be your child, your best friend, or your mother. Whoever it is, though, make it someone who holds your same convictions. If not, they could encourage you in wrong rather than right. Knowing that someone is aware of your actions and can call you on them if they become questionable is often the thing we need to keep us honest, especially if your inward, spiritual voice is being drowned out by raging hormones. You will be happy you heeded those words of caution when you experience the glory of God on your relationship.

I remember very fondly the weight of glory on my wedding day. Before the wedding began, a tornado was in the forecast. It was windy and cloudy when my limo came to pick me up. I received word that a few of my friends from out of town could not come because their flight was cancelled due to bad weather. As I rode to the church in my rented limo, I wondered if the sun was going to come out or if the sky would remain dreary. When we got to the church, I had to run inside because the wind was blowing my freshly pressed hair and soft up-do out of place. The wedding was to begin at two. It was 1:30, and my makeup artist hadn't yet arrived to do my makeup. Needless to say, I was getting antsy. Finally, my makeup was done and I was dressed. Peeking through the window into the sanctuary, I could see HIM standing there looking so handsome in a white tuxedo with a lavender boutonniere. I could also see my bridesmaids coming down the aisle.

Suddenly, I heard one of my wedding singers stop singing. He had forgotten the words to the verse. *Wow,* I thought. *I can't believe that just happened.* But all I wanted was for someone to get me out there to that man waiting for me. The doors were opened, and I was looking out into smiling faces, beautiful flowers, and my man. I stepped through the doors on my uncle's arm with a big smile on my face. The song "The One He Kept for Me" by Maurette Brown Clark was being sung, which was absolutely fitting for that moment.

About halfway down the aisle, the tears began to flow like a river. It was like the feeling of being in a deep place of worship before God where all you can do is weep before Him. I was overwhelmed that I had finally reached that moment in my life. My heart's desire was being fulfilled right before my very eyes by God himself. There was an incredible feeling of accomplishment and a humble sense of gratitude flowing from my heart that manifested as an abundant river of tears. God's presence was definitely in the room and His train had filled the temple. I know better than to believe any of that was about me. It was God rewarding me for keeping His Word, just as He would honor anyone who keeps His Word.

Another important aspect to abstaining from fleshly lusts is keeping guard of your mind and spirit. Well, how do I guard my mind and spirit, you ask? By being in control of your ear gate, your eye gate, and your mouth gate. Your ears, eyes, and mouth are gates through which spiritual information travel. This information can be beneficial or harmful, depending on the things you allow yourself to be exposed to (i.e., television programs, songs, books, conversations, etc.). It is your job to filter out negativity in the form of media that promotes promiscuity, fornication, adultery, and other sexual sins. You've got to do it because no one else will. Why is this so important? Because your testimony depends on it. I remember watching *Midnight Love* on BET as a teenager and thinking, *I wish I had a man.* Those love songs with their suggestive power had me thinking and feeling like I was lonely and in need of a man. Wrong testimony!

Everything you take into your spirit is a seed, which will grow into something bigger if not properly dealt with. Even though you may have no intentions of getting intimate with your boo before marriage, because that is what you have been feeding your spirit and mind, that is what you will be MOST tempted to do and your flesh will comply with that temptation, not resist it. Why put yourself through the torment? It's like shooting yourself in the foot. Keep in mind that there is NOTHING good in your flesh (Romans 7:18). As a matter of truth, whoever sows to his flesh will indeed reap corruption, but whoever sows to his spirit will reap everlasting life (Galatians 6:18). Whatever you allow into your ear, eye, and mouth gate will either fortify your flesh or your spirit. It is to your advantage to have a much stronger spirit so that you can defeat the enemy at every turn. Think of yourself as a soldier defending her territory. You've got on the whole armor of God, and you are ready to protect what's yours from invasion. The only thing that should invade your mind and spirit are the things found in Philippians 4:8 (KJV).

Finally, brethren, whatsoever things are true, whatsoever things are honest, whatsoever things are just, whatsoever things are pure, whatsoever things are lovely, whatsoever things are of good report; if there be any virtue, and if there be any praise, think on these things.

One of my favorite scriptures is Psalm 37:4-5 (KJV), which says, "Delight thyself also in the Lord; and he shall give thee the desires of thine heart. Commit thy way unto the Lord; trust also in him; and he shall bring it to pass." When we find pleasure in the Lord, He gives us the desires of our heart. What this means is that what He wants for us becomes what we want for ourselves, and our desires get in line with His will. Then, when we commit our lives and our day-to-day actions to Him, He brings those desires to pass. God's best and perfect mate for you in His time, in His way, all without the hassle, heartbreak, and headache…who wouldn't want that?

The Waiting Room

1. In what practical ways can you protect your ear, eye, and mouth gate?

   _____

   _____

2. What boundaries can you set in your relationships to avoid putting yourself in sexually tempting situations?

   _____

   _____

3. Name at least two trustworthy people in your life who can serve as accountability partners for you and vice versa.

   _____

   _____

 Say this confession in faith...

My body is the temple of the Holy Ghost (1 Corinthians 6:19). I present my body as a living sacrifice, holy and acceptable unto God, which is my reasonable act of service. I am not conformed to this world, but I am transformed by the renewing of my mind so that I can test and approve what is the good and acceptable and perfect will of God (Romans 12:1-2). I yield myself unto God and my members as instruments of righteousness unto God, servants to righteousness unto holiness (Romans 6:13). I am dead to sin and alive in Christ. Sin no longer reigns in my body and it has no dominion over me, for I operate under the grace of God (Romans 6:14). My body does not control me. I control it, and I command it to line up with the Word of God. I am free from sin and alive unto God. I have the mind of Christ and I will do always those things that please Him. My body belongs to God and I do with it what He commands. God is my keeper and the strength of my life. He keeps me from all manner of evil. I will lay aside every weight and the sin that so easily besets me. I run with patience the race set before me (Hebrews 12:1). I wait patiently for the husband that God has promised me and I won't awaken love until it is time. That time is when I enter into holy matrimony with the spouse God has for me. Until that day, I devote all my time, energy, and affection to the Lord, and I attend to Him without distraction. In Jesus's name.

Reflection—what does it all mean to you?

_____

_____

_____

_____

_____

_____

_____

CHAPTER 3

Involve Your Spiritual Leader

"Where no counsel is, the people fall: but in the multitude of counselors there is safety." (Proverbs 11:14 KJV)

"And I will give you pastors according to mine heart, which shall feed you with knowledge and understanding." (Jeremiah 3:15 KJV)

My pastor and his wife played a pivotal role in my relationship from the start. As a matter of fact, they were the ones who set Russell and me up. Knowing that my spiritual leaders—the ones I trust to guide me spiritually—approved of my dating choice gave me a peace of mind. The added bonus was that they pastored Russell too, so their insight proved to be a valuable tool in deciding if we were right for each other.

It was my Elect Lady (my pastor's wife) who first planted the idea for our marriage in my mind. To my husband's good fortune, Elect Lady was his cheerleader before he and I ever began dating. She knew I desired to be married and she would tell me on occasion, "Brother Whitaker is a good man. He loves his mama and his ministry." She knew the type of man I needed, and she saw it in Russell before anyone else.

It was my pastor that I went to when I needed to know what to do about my interest in getting to know Russell. He thought it would be a great idea for us to get to know each other and decided the best thing to do was let him do the talking. A few weeks later, Russell asked me out. The rest is history.

Looking back at the way our story played out makes me wonder where I would be and what condition my life would be in right now if I had not sought the counsel of my spiritual leaders or refused to listen to them at all. I really don't want to imagine that place because it wouldn't be as sweet as where I am now. I realize that my life has purpose and a visionary sees that purpose.

Have *you* ever kept a romantic relationship a secret? Why was that? What some Christian women tend to do is avoid introducing their dating partner to their spiritual leader or parents until things get serious. Maybe they are private and don't want anyone in their business. Maybe they are ashamed of their guy's social, financial, or physical status. Maybe they just don't want to jinx it by revealing the relationship too soon. But the danger in withholding this information from key people is that by the time you finally get around to it, you are more than likely blinded by love and less likely to hear constructive criticism about that new person in your life. The things that may have presented themselves as red flags at first have become tolerable or disguised by rose-colored glasses. In other words, you are sprung—head-over-heels for someone who you might come to realize is not the Prince Charming you first envisioned! Had your pastor been involved from the beginning, before you invested so much time and emotion into your relationship, his or her wise counsel might have been better received. Parting ways, if necessary, would be much easier to do, and your heart would be protected from the hurt that often comes from doing things *your way*. Proverbs 11:14 (KJV) states, "Where no counsel is, the people fall: but in the multitude of counselors there is safety." Proverbs 15:22 (KJV) echoes this with, "Without counsel, purposes are disappointed: but in the multitude of counselors they are established." Seeking counsel from those with your best interest and God's will at heart is for your benefit. You don't want to have regrets later. Now, I am not saying that everything will be perfect if you receive counsel. However, I am saying that getting insight helps you establish a solid foundation upon which to continue building your relationship.

What Every Single Woman Should Know to Receive God's Best!

The mistake that many make is in hiding their less-than-perfect sweetie—well, because they *are* less than perfect! Christian women know that according to God's Word, there are certain qualities we should seek in a mate: kindness, gentleness, honesty, integrity, and faithfulness. All of these involve a man's character—that which he does when no one is looking. Unfortunately, when desire turns to lust, many women will accept just about anything as long as it means that they have someone they can call theirs. "He can change," they say to try and justify hanging in there. At this point, many are afraid that their spiritual leader will see the same faults they're trying to ignore, and they don't want to be confronted with that truth. Denial is a coping mechanism for the problem you know exists, so letting that objective party counsel you keeps you in the safety zone. It's the accountability we all need to keep us on track.

Let's assume you go ahead and marry that person with the excess baggage instead of heeding the warnings of those who love you. Who will you go to for counsel to talk about the problems that have gone from molehills to mountains? You will probably expect your pastor to pray for you and give you a word to overcome these problems, and he or she will do it because that's their responsibility to you and the rest of the flock of God.

I liken this to having a car repaired. I once owned a car that I absolutely loved. It was my first car purchase and the car that taught me how to drive a stick shift. On top of that—it was paid for! I even planned to pass that car onto my kids one day. Well, that will never happen now because of a poor decision I made in having it repaired. It needed a new muffler, and it was also time to have the timing belt changed. Originally, I took it to a reputable mechanic in town to get his assessment, but I didn't like his price—at all. "I'm not paying that!" I said. "I can get someone else to do it cheaper." Well, as it turned out, the price was very fair according to another mechanic I spoke to, because apparently timing belts can be very complicated to replace. But I didn't want to accept that, so I took my dear automobile to a friend I knew (not a licensed mechanic) who promised he could handle the repairs for a fraction of the cost I'd been quoted.

 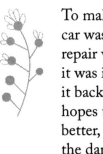

If you just listen to the spiritual leaders in your life and trust their guidance, you will be much better off and able to avoid some very costly repairs to your heart.

To make a long story short, my car wasn't the same after the repair work was done. Actually, it was in worse condition. I took it back to the first mechanic in hopes that he could make it all better, and he did his best, but the damage had already been done. The lesson that I learned was to take my vehicles to the experts, trust their advice, and allow them to do what they are trained for—NOT expect them to fix an out-of-control mess that wouldn't have even happened if I'd just listened to their advice in the first place! Had I followed their instructions and let them do the work to begin with, I'd probably still have my car today, but that one decision cost me more in the end than the mechanic's original price. I had to pay for the shoddy work, the work to fix the damage done, and after my poor car finally kept conking out on me, I had to buy another! Dear heart, I hope you can understand how this relates to receiving and following divine counsel for your life. If you just listen to the spiritual leaders in your life and trust their guidance, you will be much better off and able to avoid some very costly repairs to your heart.

A scene from the movie *Courageous* illustrates this point beautifully. The African-American police officer was concerned about his daughter's dating choices. He thought she was too young to date and didn't want her dating just anybody. The daughter thought her father was being too overprotective and wanted to ruin her fun. What she didn't realize was that her dad had more insight than she gave him credit for. As it turned out, the guy she was interested in ended up hanging with the wrong crowd and was arrested on drug charges. Here's where the tears began to flow for me: the young girl's father took her to a nice restaurant for dinner, gave her a ring, and told her the sweetest, most beautiful things—that she was precious to him and he wanted her to allow him to help her choose her mate at the right time. Why was he qualified to do this? Well, he was her father and knew her best and had her best interests in mind. Being a man also helped him identify a good man when he saw one.

Allowing a godly, earthly father and/or a spiritual father like that of a pastor to be involved in the dating process from the beginning is a true sign of trust in his care for you. Since my natural father passed when I was just a baby, I placed my trust in the hands of my spiritual leader to guide me in life's major decisions. And who can do that job better than God's chosen representative? If he or she is truly after God's heart (like my pastor), the heart of God for you will show in their counsel. It's not their job to tell you what to do—it's to advise you on God's will. And don't forget, it's still your decision whether to follow that advice or not. But let me remind you that following is an act of obedience, and obedience is the doorway to blessings. Had I been advised against starting a relationship with my husband, it would have been easier to walk away from a potentially bad situation because it was before any feelings and time were invested in the relationship.

What's also risky about not seeking or heeding counsel is not experiencing the infinitely wise best from God, only your own finite best. When your best proves to be a washout, it's then that many people resort to counseling. But why not head the mess off from the start and begin with advice from those you trust? I know you may be thinking that God said He'd give you the desires of your heart, and He will. But are those desires ordained and inspired by God? If not, you may just end up with what you asked for, which isn't what you really need. You've got lots of options available to you, but not every option will profit you.

Think about these options: you can either have love *and* marriage or love *or* marriage. This reminds me of those State Farm commercials that talk about dividing commonly known pairs like sweet-and-sour chicken, wet-and-wild water parks, etc. If you refuse counsel from someone cautioning you against getting into a relationship that isn't good for you, you could end up in an either/or situation. Instead of love and marriage, you could end up with love or marriage—marriage without the fulfilling and unconditional love shared between a husband and wife. This type of marriage is devoid of love's qualities found in 1 Corinthians 13. It lacks trust, patience, kindness, commitment, sacrifice, forgiveness, and gentleness. This marriage is like a business arrangement, with each person trying to get something from the other rather than it being a partnership and lifelong journey. That is not God's original intent for marriage.

In fact, before creating a woman for man, He said that it was not good for man to be alone. The sad reality is that many married people still find themselves alone—even with another person in the house—because the emotional connection is not there. It is the absolute truth that God can restore and rebuild broken relationships, and His love does cover a multitude of sins, but wouldn't it be better to avoid the pitfall to begin with?

Someone told me about a couple who went to their pastor for advice about their relationship after they decided to marry. The pastor told the two of them that they were not ready for marriage, but in private he told the young lady (a member of his church) that the man she was dating was not her husband, and he refused to marry them because of this. Well, the couple didn't receive that word too well and decided to get married elsewhere. Where is that relationship now? Divorced. The so-called "love of her life" became abusive after they married. Wow! They say hindsight is 20/20, and I bet that if that poor woman knew then what she knows now, she would have gone a different direction. I also bet she wishes that she had listened to her spiritual leader from the beginning and considered his point of view. Since we're talking about sight and point of view, let's also consider another benefit of consulting your spiritual leader. He or she has vision. Not only can they hear from God on another level, they can also see on another level.

Let's take Moses for example. He was the great leader called by God to lead the children of Israel out of Egypt into the Promised Land. You know the story: after the Passover, Pharaoh finally decided to let the Israelites go. However, while they were on their way, Pharaoh's heart became hardened again. What did he do? He went back on his word. As Pharaoh's army pursued the Israelites in the desert, they all reached a great barrier—the Red Sea. A decision had to be made. Where would they go? Would they turn back around and surrender to the Egyptians? Would they fight? Would they choose to die in the sea rather than to become enslaved again?

The Israelites began to murmur and complain. In my mind's eye, I can see Moses saying to himself, "We ain't going out like that!" Moses didn't choose any of these options because he had heard from God, and He revealed a different way of escape that no one else could.

"And Moses stretched out his hand over the sea and the Lord caused the sea to go back by a strong east wind all that night, and made the sea dry land, and the waters were divided" (Exodus 14:21 KJV).

Where the people saw water, God revealed to Moses dry land. Where they saw death, God showed Moses life. Where the people saw hopelessness, God revealed to Moses a great opportunity, and Moses decided that with God's help, he and the Israelites would cross to the other side of the sea. It was Moses' job to reveal what the rest of the people couldn't see, and we even see later that it was Moses who went to the mountaintop to speak with God.

Face it—the view is always better from the top. It reveals much more territory and lets you see further into the distance. The Word of God speaks for itself in Proverbs 29:18 when it says, "Where there is no vision, the people perish." If Moses hadn't had the vision to see the possibilities and the faith to believe God to part the seas, the people could have indeed died.

But the word *perish* doesn't just mean to die a physical death. It also means to loosen and to go back. Many of the Israelites were willing to loosen their hold on freedom and go back into captivity when faced with what seemed like the insurmountable challenge of the sea and Pharaoh's army. What does this mean for you and me? We also need a leader with a God-vision to push us forward in the right direction. If we look at the obstacles surrounding us—our age, the limited dating pool, our biological clocks (holler when I'm on your doorstep)—we can be tempted to perish by loosening our grip on God's promises and "going back" into meaningless, aimless, commitment-less, and peace-less relationships. Sometimes, we need help to see God's plan for us.

Word to the wise—if you and your boo attend the same church, then the pastor knows both individuals and should be able to tell if you would make a good match or not. If you attend different churches, then soon after the dating begins (but before those three little words are spoken), introduce him to your leader to let him or her feel him out first. And be ready to receive what they say. You can save yourself a lot of time, heartache, and embarrassment down the road.

 The Waiting Room

1. Have you ever hidden a romantic relationship from the important people in your life for fear of criticism?

   _____

   _____

2. What will you do differently to get sound spiritual counsel about your romantic relationships?

   _____

   _____

3. How will getting counsel from your spiritual leader help you get God's best?

   _____

   _____

 Say this confession in faith...

The counsel of the Lord shall stand and in the multitude of counselors there is safety (Proverbs 11:14). I trust in God's counsel and His chosen vessels. God has given me a pastor after His own heart to feed me with knowledge and understanding and to give me divine counsel. Under my pastor's teaching, I am being perfected, edified and made more and more into the image of Christ. I am no longer tossed to and fro or carried about by every wind of doctrine, by the sleight of men and cunning craftiness whereby men lie in wait to deceive (Ephesians 4:14). I do not trust in horses or chariots, but I trust in the Lord. I heed God's counsel through my pastor because he/she speaks the Word of faith and the Word of truth with his/her mouth. My pastor has my best interest at heart. I will be forthcoming about my dating relationships with those who watch for my soul before my heart is invested, so that I can remain in the place of safety, and that is in the will of God. In Jesus's name.

Reflection—*what does it all mean to you?*

_____

_____

_____

_____

_____

_____

_____

_____

CHAPTER 4

Trim Your List

"But the Lord said unto Samuel, Look not on his countenance,
or on the height of his stature; because I have refused him: for
the Lord seeth not as man seeth; for man looketh on the outward
appearance, but the Lord looketh on the heart."
(1 Samuel 16:7 KJV)

Isn't it just like God to tell us that what is on the outside isn't important when everything in the world tells us it is? Fitness centers are packed with people trying to get and keep their bodies in shape (me included). Department stores run sale after sale to get you to buy the latest fashions. And don't get me started on the media. False perceptions of beauty are everywhere you look. But my encouragement to you is this—when it comes to waiting for a life partner, stick to what is most important. What's most important is not what's in his wallet or draped on his back. It's what's in his heart. While money and attraction are important, and both have their place within a marriage, they should not be the ultimate deciding factor in choosing a mate. Money alone will not make a man have integrity, but integrity can bring a fortune into his possession.

Consider how King David was chosen. After the Lord rejected Saul from the position of king, He sent the prophet Samuel to Jesse's house to find and anoint his successor. I imagine Samuel and Jesse sitting together as if at a fashion show, waiting for the male models to grace the stage. First up was Eliab. He was tall and handsome and, being the oldest son, he was probably more responsible than the rest. "Oh, surely he's the one!" exclaimed Samuel. But God said not so. "It ain't all about his looks. It's about what's in his heart, so keep it moving." Up next was Abinadab, then Shammah, then seven other sons. But none of them fit the bill either! "Are these all of your sons?" asked Samuel. "I have my youngest son named David, but he's tending to the sheep," replied Jesse. Samuel responded, "Go get him because I'm not leaving until you do." Then, here comes David. Now David, he was definitely an unlikely choice. He was Jesse's youngest son and a shepherd boy to boot. Choose the lowest guy on the totem pole to rule a nation? Who does that? God, that's who. To Him, David was a diamond in the rough because David had the right heart for the job. All the exterior qualities and refinement would come— sort of like on-the-job training.

Now for even more compelling evidence to support God's choice, let's take a closer look at the candidates for king. Eliab's name means "God of his father." Break it down to its parts and you get "El" which means "strength, mighty, goodly, great, idol, and power" and "Ab" which means "father and chief." Please allow me to use my imagination again for a moment. This is the guy with all the money, power, and respect. The CEO and head honcho, if you will. Be careful not to idolize men like this. They could have so much power that they develop a god-like complex and feel they are in control of everything—even you. It doesn't matter how strong he is physically (hey, I can appreciate a great physique too!), or how much power and influence he may have. He may lack the ability to value you in his effort to maintain his powerful status.

Abinadab is another interesting guy. His name means "father of generosity." This is the guy who feels he can buy your love with flashy gifts and expensive dinners—the Sugar Daddy. Ladies, it doesn't matter how much stuff he gives you. When the gifts stop coming, then what? If the bank account gets low, and sometimes it does, then what? Will you still love him in the absence of stuff? No gift can substitute for true, genuine, unconditional love, so don't get caught up in him either.

Shammah means "astonishment and desolation"—a very perplexing combination. This is the guy who knows all the right things to say, but can't back any of it up—the Mack Daddy. Maybe he doesn't have much to offer in the looks department, but he sure makes up for it with his silver tongue. But it doesn't matter how astonishingly charming he is, because charm is deceitful and beauty is vain according to Proverbs 31:30 (KJV). Don't be deceived by his words because, in many cases, they don't mean a thing except as a way to get you to give him what he wants and afterwards leave you high and dry. Leave this dude in the dust!

While money and attraction are important, and both have their place within a marriage, they should not be the ultimate deciding factor in choosing a mate. Money alone will not make a man have integrity, but integrity can bring a fortune into his possession.

Finally, we get to David. Now the name David means "loving." This is the guy who knows how to treat a woman—our Mr. Right. He has the right heart and a love for God. And, because of his love for God, he can love you according to God's instructions—the way you need and deserve to be loved! David also had a good name among others. A servant of Saul had this to say about him in 1 Samuel 16:18 (KJV): "I have seen a son of Jesse the Bethlehemite, that is cunning in playing, and a mighty valiant man, and a man of war, and prudent in matters, and a comely person, and the Lord is with him." That is the kind of man you want by your side—the kind of man who can rule a kingdom and a family in a way that is pleasing to God. David may have started out with meager means and a humble job, but he ended up a wealthy ruler. Talk about a promotion! Maybe the man God has for you has or will have a similar testimony. I believe mine will.

At present, I make more money than my husband. That, to some women, is a deal breaker. It isn't for me. My husband is so generous with what he does have. He has no problem sharing his income with me, and I still consider him a provider because of that. About two years before I met my husband, my pastor prophesied to me that God would send me a good man. It took two years and a few counterfeits, but my pastor's word did not return to him void. My husband is indeed a good man. He has an amazing heart and is full of the qualities that God sets out as true marks of His children. But I wouldn't have known it if I hadn't given him the opportunity and invested in him—regardless of his bank account!

What some women fail to realize is that relationships are also investments. We invest time, energy, money, and emotions when we become involved in them. Consider this analogy: small, new companies are cheaper than large, well-established ones. You can buy low and then make millions when it takes off. Coming in on the ground floor of a company has its advantages. By the time it is really successful, you will be in one of the top paid positions. Here's the connection. Let's say the guy on your "list" is Walmart, or some large, famous company. Everybody wants a piece, which means more competition and more women vying for his attention. The guy who only meets a few of your requirements is like the small, new company. No one is paying any attention to him, but with your love, help, and support, he could rise to the top in no time.

Case in point—after a little encouragement from me, my husband has decided to go back to school to better himself and provide more for the family. I know that the Lord touched his heart on the matter because he was perfectly content with his current job, but he has a desire to be more of a provider and has learned that he has to step out on faith in order to receive more income. God is not just going to deliver the money to his doorstep—he has to go get it! And I am proud because I know that he is doing it for us. Now that we are married, he has more favor than ever on his life because of God's promise. Remember what Proverbs 18:22 (KJV) says: "He that findeth a wife findeth a good thing and obtaineth favor from the Lord." So, no, he didn't have the large salary when we met, but he had the right heart. Now I get to experience, play a part in, and benefit from the man he is becoming.

My advice to you, my sister, is to be selective but not prejudicial, which is judging someone too harshly before getting to know him. That guy you keep passing over could be a diamond in the rough, but you'll never know that if you stick to your rigid, almost-always-impossible-to-achieve list. I'm not promoting settling or aiming lower. Just remember to aim for the important things. Our expectations should definitely be high, but not so high that they border on perfection. Have you reached perfection? No matter how fabulous you are, there is still room to grow.

So what if he's not 6'2"? What if his hair isn't curly just like you like it? What if he is a shade darker than you had planned? Do those things determine how happy you'll be or how successful your marriage will be? I'd venture to say that they wouldn't.

My last bit of encouragement here is to open your mind to new possibilities. Sometimes we can't see the forest for the trees. What exactly does that mean? It means to be overwhelmed by detail to the point where it obscures the overall situation. Had I remained rigid in my assessment of a good man, I would have missed out on my one truly good thing! My initial hang-up with my husband was his age. I said several times in the past that the fifteen years between us was a deal breaker. I never once considered dating someone so much older than me! It was, quite frankly, a turnoff to begin with, but now it is a non-issue. When I actually took the time to get to know Russell, I was blown away with how much we actually had in common. We get along great (almost as if we were the same age), and the years of experience have only made him a better, more patient man—just what I need. Honestly, I can't see myself with anyone else because we are a perfect match.

Matches made in heaven must obviously be maintained on earth, but the Word of God makes the maintenance easier to perform. Stay in the Word and see if it won't cause your love to grow in knowledge and help you know what is vital and important in a marriage relationship. (Philippians1:9-10).

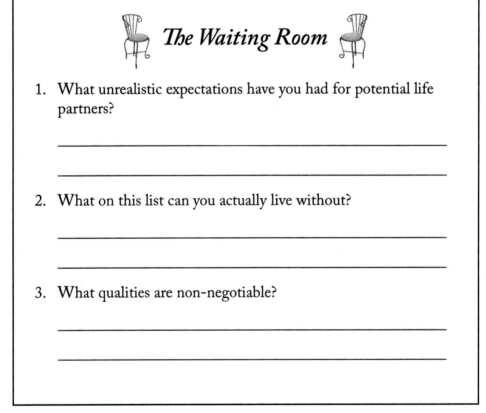

The Waiting Room

1. What unrealistic expectations have you had for potential life partners?

   _____

   _____

2. What on this list can you actually live without?

   _____

   _____

3. What qualities are non-negotiable?

   _____

   _____

4. What will you do to improve yourself while you're waiting?

_____

_____

Say this confession in faith...

My love abounds more and more in knowledge and in all judgment (Philippians 1:9). I see others the way that God sees them, after the heart. I am not so hung up on a man's looks that I overlook his character. I will not be consumed by shallow expectations or things that fade away with time. The man that God sends me will possess long-lasting qualities like kindness, humility, integrity, and honesty. My priorities are right because they are in line with God's Word. He has given me the desires of my heart. My desire for a godly husband is from Him, and as I commit my way to the Lord, He will bring my desires to pass. God has someone designed especially for me, and I will wait in faith for his arrival. In Jesus's name.

Reflections—what does it all mean to you?

_____

_____

_____

_____

_____

CHAPTER 5

Own God's Promises

"Let us hold fast the profession of our faith without wavering; (for he is faithful that promised)..." (Hebrews 10:23 KJV)

"Cast not away therefore your confidence, which hath great recompence of reward." (Hebrews 10:35 KJV)

Ownership carries a great deal of weight in our society. It's the American Dream, and a rite of passage into adulthood, to own your own piece of property. I was twenty-five years old when I bought my first home. I felt empowered, accomplished, and more adult-like than ever. I could have just rented an apartment, but I figured if I was going to pay, I might as well pay for it to someday be mine. To me it seemed like renting was pouring my money down the drain and, in much the same way, so is choosing not to believe or own God's promises for you. Not following God's will or seeking His guidance in any area, including your marital status, is a waste of God's goodness.

Let me explain how these things relate. One reason that a person would choose to rent is because they don't want the responsibility that comes with homeownership, such as paying for costly repairs. Another reason is because he or she only plans to occupy the property temporarily, so no need to make the major investment. And in many cases, because of this lack of responsibility, renters don't value the property as much as an owner would. That's housing with convenience, wouldn't you say? Well, convenience isn't always a good thing. While the renter has less responsibility for the property, they don't get to experience the benefits that

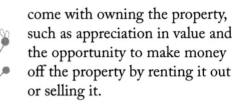

When situations and circumstances try to make you doubt, you must say what God says. Let me be clear. When you speak the language of faith you are not speaking your own words. You are speaking God's Words, and His Words have power!

come with owning the property, such as appreciation in value and the opportunity to make money off the property by renting it out or selling it.

What's the connection to standing on God's Word? Believers should not believe the Word temporarily, only when conditions look favorable. That makes you double-minded and unstable in all your ways (James 1:22). Instead, we should value the Word of God and take ownership of it. Owning God's promises, which are found in His Word, means you believe you have them, even if you cannot see them. That's faith. Then we will be able to reap the benefits it offers. So how do you own it? By believing it, confessing it, and defending it.

Belief in God's Word is where it all starts. That's how you became saved in the first place! Romans 10:9-10 (KJV) says, "If thou shalt confess with thy mouth the Lord Jesus, and shalt believe in thine heart that God hath raised him from the dead, thou shalt be saved." Verse eleven goes on to say that, "…whosoever believeth on him shall not be ashamed." I am convinced that this not only works for salvation, but for anything you desire from the Lord according to His Word—including a mate. This is the faith process. God makes a promise, and we live our lives based on those promises, even though we may not have any tangible proof of their existence. We believe in our heart of hearts that they are true. Again, your salvation is a perfect example. Every Christian believes in God whom they have never seen, and they believe that they are saved and will go to heaven one day, even though they've never been there; and it's because we believe God's promises. *Anything* you believe, you can receive. When we believe God's Word, He moves on our behalf to prove that He keeps His Word. He wants you to know that He "is not a man that he should lie; neither the son of man, that he should repent: hath he said, and shall he not do it? or hath he spoken, and shall he not make it good?" (Numbers 23:19 KJV). His part is to perform the work. Your part is to believe on Him. God's Word is full of juicy promises. It's part of your inheritance, so why not claim it?

Confessing His Word, as previously stated, is a sign of your belief and another element to the process of faith. When situations and circumstances try to make you doubt, you must say what God says. Let me be clear. When you speak the language of faith, you are not speaking your own words. You are speaking God's Words, and His Words have power! They are so powerful that the world and everything in it was created by them. (Hebrews 11:3) My dear sister, God's Word spoken out of *your* mouth has that same creative power to cause things that do not exist to come into being. That's right. You were made in His image and in His likeness, so you share your Father's traits (Genesis 1:26). Still not convinced that your words have power? Don't take my word for it. Here's what the Bible has to say.

"Death and life are in the power of the tongue, and they that love it shall eat the fruit thereof." (Proverbs 18:21 KJV)

You can either speak death to your situation by saying things like "I'll never get married" or "nobody wants to marry me" or you can speak life by confessing God's word. I never said this would be easy or that it would happen overnight, hence the words "faith *process*." Undoubtedly, you will experience some hardship and suffering because of your belief, but the more you saturate yourself in His promises toward you, the more your belief is solidified. Romans 10:17 shows us that faith comes by hearing and hearing by the Word of God, so confessing the Word causes you to hear it over and over and over again. What happens then? Your faith increases. The more faith you have, the more you please God. The more you please God through faith and obedience, the more He rewards your faith and obedience. It is so worth the time and dedication to consistently confess the Word over your life.

Lastly, defend the Word. Don't let anything make you doubt it, not distractions, not naysayers, not anything. Do NOT change your confession no matter what criticism you face. If the devil knows that you are not firm in your belief, he will try his best to evict you from your place of blessing. Do not allow him to do it! The best example that comes to my mind is Peter in Matthew 14:28. Peter stepped out on faith (and literally onto the open water) after Jesus told him to come. He did not hesitate to do it because he believed he could. But when he became distracted by the boisterous winds and waves, Peter began to fear. He was light as a feather, but his wavering faith turned him into a boulder, sinking him to the bottom of the sea. Jesus saved him, but He also asked an important question: "Why did you doubt?" Beloved, protect your faith from doubt at all costs. God's best for you depends on it.

God's Word is explicit in Mark 11:24 (KJV) when it says, "What things soever ye desire when ye pray, believe that ye receive them and ye shall have them." 1 John 5:14-15 (KJV) also states, "And this is the confidence that we have in him, that, if we ask anything according to his will, he heareth us: and if we know that he hear us, whatsoever we ask, we know that we have the petitions that we desired of him." That sounds like free access to whatever you want to me. Wait, let me qualify that last statement. The "whatever you want" must be in line with His will. Wanting someone else's husband is not in line with His will, so don't even think about asking for that. God will not do it. He will, on the other hand, honor your belief in His Word and give you a man that meets His qualifications and yours.

The Waiting Room

1. What does it mean to own God's promises?

   _____

   _____

2. What is your plan to incorporate consistent confession into your life?

   _____

   _____

3. How will you defend God's promises to you in the midst of opposition?

   _____

   _____

 Say this confession in faith...

What things soever I desire when I pray, I believe that I receive them and I shall have them. And this is the confidence that I have in Him, that, if I ask anything *according to His will*, he hears me; and if I know that He hears me, whatsoever I ask, I know that I have the petitions that I desire of him (1 John 5:14-15). I desire to be married, and I know that God ordained marriage; therefore, it is good and pleasing to God. I am a virtuous woman and my price is far above rubies. The heart of my husband safely trusts in me, for I do him good and not evil all the days of my life (Proverbs 31:11). It is not good for man to dwell alone, so I believe that I am a helpmate (suitable help) for the man that God has chosen for me. The desire of my heart is from God, and He will bring it to pass. I will be a prudent wife and a good thing to the man who finds me. My husband and I shall live joyfully together and in love all the days of our lives. In Jesus's name.

Reflections—what does it all mean to you?

_____

_____

_____

_____

_____

_____

_____

CHAPTER 6

Never Compromise

"Give not that which is holy to the dogs, neither cast ye your pearls before swine, lest they trample them under their feet, and turn again and rend you." (Matthew 7:6 KJV)

Have you ever had someone challenge your beliefs? I did—a man I met who challenged me about attending church. From our very first conversation, he could tell that I valued spirituality, and I never tried to hide that fact. After that, he wanted to go with me to church immediately. Personally, I thought it was a little soon, but I went with it, thinking that if a soul came to Christ, it would be worth it. Well, come to Christ he did—at least, according to him. I guess he thought that doing so would have me hooked. He confessed salvation on the first visit to Bible study. I wasn't as hooked as he'd hoped, but I stuck in there to see what would come of this encounter. He came to church with me a few more times but, after a few weeks, he could no longer maintain the charade.

I noticed that, all of a sudden, he stopped calling me. After several attempts to find out the cause of this behavior, he revealed the depths of his heart—he thought I went to church too much, and wished that I would take a break occasionally to do other things, like go out with him. I couldn't believe his complaint. "Would you rather I spend most of my time in the club or something?" I asked. His response: "Well, no, but at least make a compromise for me." Compromise?! I had only known him for a matter of weeks and here he was, asking me to alter my spiritual convictions to accommodate him! I don't think so! But just when I thought he had revealed the worst, he said, "That's why church girls can't

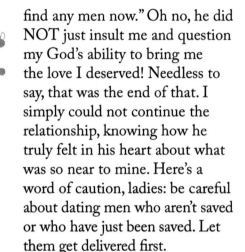

> **He needs to see your standards so he can decide if he is able to meet them. Lowering your standards now can lead to him not taking you or your standards seriously later in the relationship.**

find any men now." Oh no, he did NOT just insult me and question my God's ability to bring me the love I deserved! Needless to say, that was the end of that. I simply could not continue the relationship, knowing how he truly felt in his heart about what was so near to mine. Here's a word of caution, ladies: be careful about dating men who aren't saved or who have just been saved. Let them get delivered first.

On another occasion, I made the decision not to leave my church for love or money. You might think that decision strange, but I knew that was where I was supposed to be. God had planted me there, and when I tried to go elsewhere for convenience sake, He reminded me in a very real way that He had already put me where He wanted me to be—period. That was where my spiritual nourishment would be provided and where I'd grow into a mature believer. And since God wasn't changing His mind about that, who was I to go against it? Hence my decision to stay, no matter what. Even though the odds seemed severely out of my favor (after all, there were very few single men in my church), I didn't leave. I played around with the thought, but God honored my commitment and the cry of my heart and sent my husband to me.

That being said, your values are valuable and should be respected. Stick with what you know was right before you met the man you're dating. If church attendance, seed sowing, and abstinence were a priority before you met him, it should remain a priority after the fact as well! He needs to see your standards so he can decide if he is able to meet them. Lowering your standards now can lead to him not taking you or your standards seriously later in the relationship.

Let's use sexual intercourse as an example. How can a woman try to get a man to go to church on Sunday after sleeping with him Saturday night, and then complain that he won't go and doesn't find living for God important? What message is that sending him? Do you yourself find living for God important? Let's not have double standards here. How is your man to believe that you are serious about your walk with God if you aren't living it out on a day-to-day basis? And trust me, just because someone is a churchgoer doesn't mean that he or she has a heart for God. Jesus illustrated this point in addressing the Pharisees and Sadducees. Jesus said in Matthew 15:8 (KJV), "This people draweth nigh unto me with their mouth, and honoureth me with their lips; but their heart is far from me." Anyone who has a heart for the things of God endeavors to do His will and obey him. Christ also says that, "…if ye love me, keep my commandments" (John 14:15 KJV). So if you are not keeping God's commandments, why are you expecting different from your man? It is your clean lifestyle that will win him over, not nagging or a misleading example (1 Peter 3:1-2).

And be mindful that the person you're interested in is not attempting to meet your standards for a limited time only. Some men will put on a Dr. Jekyll face, doing what you expect or what they think makes you happy, but this only lasts up to a certain point (usually just until they think they have your devotion). Then, here comes Mr. Hyde! But by then, many women end up settling because they don't want to go through the embarrassment of a failed relationship or the hassle of starting over with a new one. Many people also find that if they've had unsuccessful relationships in the past, they're also more conditioned to expect the worst in every future relationship. This negative thinking prevents any of us from expecting the love God has promised us. A good friend of mine once said that the reasons people stop pursuing God's promises is because of a fear of failure; a fear of rejection; a fear of feeling that they are not good enough; and a fear of feeling like they're too late or unqualified. But my sister, those are all tactics of Satan to get you to forfeit God's best for you. Yes, I said forfeit. Don't forget, Satan doesn't have the authority to just take anything from you. He's waiting for you to give up and give in. Don't.

Don't feel as if you should water down your standards to "help" God meet them. He is more than "able to do exceedingly abundantly above all we ask or think, according to the power that worketh in us" (Ephesians 3:20 KJV). Just ask Abraham. His wife (Sarah) thought God needed her help to make him the father of many nations, so she got Hagar (her handmaid) to lay with Abraham (what was she thinking?) so that Hagar could have a child for him. But Hagar and Ishmael (Abraham's son through Hagar) were not the promise. It could have been that Sarah doubted her own ability to bring forth a son because of her age and physical condition, but God knew all of that before he told Abraham about the good news! God is able to do what we see is the impossible. Just think—if God can bless the womb of an elderly woman to fulfill His promise, how easy it is for him to bring you the love you've been waiting for?

Job also never lowered his standards, even though people around him said things contrary to his faith. His own wife asked him, "Dost thou still retain thine integrity? Curse God and die" (Job 2:9 KJV). In other words, she was asking, "Are you crazy? Our children and everything we ever owned are gone, and you're still serving the God that allowed it all to happen? Just give it up, Job!" But Job responded accurately when he pointed out the foolishness of her words, and he would have been a fool to heed her words. Despite the doubts of his wife and his closest friends, Job maintained his integrity. He believed in God and held fast to that belief no matter what opposition he faced. In the end, Job receive a double portion of everything he lost. In order to receive God's best, we, too, must adopt Job's tenacity.

If you desire to be married and believe that you deserve God's best, then don't allow any man or woman to downplay that or make you change your view. If you're in that situation with the man in your life, give him an ultimatum and stick to it. You are worth the ring and everything that goes with it. So make him pay the price for you. Don't you know that you are more valuable than rubies? Proverbs 31:10 says, "Who can find a virtuous woman for her price is far above rubies" (KJV). In my research, I learned that a one-carat ruby is worth twice as much as a one-carat diamond. That's impressive! Yet, what's more impressive is that a virtuous woman is worth twice as much as that! And that's the woman I challenge you to be as you wait on God's promises to you.

The Waiting Room

1. In what ways have you been tempted to lower your standards for a man?

   _____

   _____

2. What will you do differently now that you know what you are worth?

   _____

   _____

Say this confession in faith...

The Word of God is the standard by which I live. I hear it, believe it, and I do what it says. I will hold fast to my profession for it has great recompense of reward. I will be faithful unto death to the things of God. I am not moved by my situation or my circumstances. No matter what the test, I'll not move to the left nor to the right, but I will remain firmly fixed on God's Word. I shall not be moved and I will not be shaken off the foundation of what I believe. I will maintain my integrity and continue in the things of God. I will not be deceived by counterfeits, for I wait on God's best. God's Word is the anchor of my soul. It keeps me rooted, grounded, and settled in God's will. I have the tenacity of Job to trust God, no matter what I see contrary to what I believe. I resist doubt in myself, and I resist the doubtful words of others concerning my situation. I believe God, and I will uphold the standards of His Word without compromise. In Jesus's name.

Reflections

Value line
Diamonds < Rubies < You, the virtuous woman

What does this value line mean to you?

_____

_____

_____

_____

_____

_____

CHAPTER 7

Get and Stay Busy

"Be steadfast, unmoveable, always abounding in the work of the Lord." (1 Corinthians 15:58 KJV)

"See then that ye walk circumspectly, not as fools, but as wise, redeeming the time, because the days are evil. Wherefore be ye not unwise, but understanding what the will of the Lord is."
(Ephesians 5:15-17 KJV)

Have you ever wondered why the people who take your order in a restaurant and bring your food are called waiters? Well, it's because they wait on you, but not by sitting in a corner, staring at you as they wait for you to finish your food. They serve you, bringing you what you want, the way you want it, and doing it with a smile—hopefully. Anything less than that is poor service. This is the best example of what it means to wait on God. Waiting on God does not mean twiddling your thumbs, sitting still, or pacing back and forth until He fulfills all of your wishes. God is not a genie in a bottle, so please don't reduce him to that. Waiting on Him means serving him. Psalms 27:14 (KJV) tells us, "Wait on the Lord: be of good courage, and he shall strengthen thine heart: wait, I say, on the Lord."

I always enjoy listening to the radio broadcast *Redeeming the Time* by Rick Grubbs. He has the most insightful commentary on making the most of our time as Christians. So much of our lives are wasted on meaningless activities like television, social media, and other time zappers. It's important that the single Christian learn to redeem the time they have too.

What Every Single Woman Should Know to Receive God's Best!

I wonder if the invalid man at the pool of Bethesda in John 5:2-15 redeemed his time. This man had been sick for thirty-eight years and was waiting to be healed. It was a custom that an angel would come down at certain seasons to trouble the water, and the first person to step down in it would be made whole of his disease. While the Bible doesn't indicate how long the invalid man actually lay by that pool waiting, I can imagine it had been quite some time. The Bible suggests that this man had tried to be the first one in before but had been unsuccessful—probably more than once because, "Whosoever then first after the troubling of the water stepped in was made whole of whatsoever disease he had" (John 5:4 KJV). It sounds to me like a survival-of-the-fittest situation, and unfortunately, this happens in the single world as well.

But back to the story: Jesus, knowing the man's condition and how long he'd been lying there, asked him if he wanted to be made whole. Of course, he wanted it; otherwise, he would not have been there. However, the man didn't even answer the question posed to him. Instead he said, "Sir, I have no man, when the water is troubled, to put me into the pool: but while I am coming, another steppeth down before me" (John 5: 7 KJV). His reason for not being whole was that he was waiting on a *man* to help him achieve the wholeness promised by helping him get to the water. Yes, ladies, I emphasized the word "man" for a reason. How many of us have thought that we needed a man to make us feel whole? Just like the people competing for healing, some single women also compete for the same man or to be married sooner than another. The scripture tells us in Colossians 2:10 (KJV) that "ye are complete in Him, which is the head of all principality and power." You're not complete in a husband; you're not complete in a job; you're not even complete in yourself. Remember, always remember, that you are only ever complete in Christ Jesus, and Jesus doesn't want you to wait any longer.

Jesus gave three instructions to the invalid man at the pool of Bethesda that I believe are also relevant to those waiting for husbands: Rise, take up thy bed, and walk. First, the word *rise*, according to the Greek dictionary, means to waken or rouse from sleep, from sitting or lying, from disease, from death, from obscurity (sounds like low self-esteem to me), from inactivity, from ruins, and from non-existence. In other words, quit lying around and moping about being single! Be productive with your time.

Second, Jesus commanded the man to "take up thy bed," which means to remove and put away the thing that has been holding you back. This could be your self-doubt, your low self-esteem, your despair at not having someone, etc. Whatever negative thinking you might be entertaining, follow Christ's commands and put it away!

And finally, when Jesus commanded the invalid man to walk, he meant for him to finally live and become occupied with other things aside from his condition. In other words, he meant for him to find his purpose. Impotent means weak, and my dear sister, you are not weak, so don't act as if you are. Get up! Walk in Christ! Find your purpose outside of a relationship before you find your place within one! And get this: after the man was made whole by Jesus, he was found in the temple. Whether or not he was working or worshipping there, I don't know, but the important thing is that he was in the right place to receive instructions for his new life.

You should never put your life on hold while waiting on a mate. Do the things that make you happy and fulfilled! Increase the level of your service in ministry. The busier you are about our Father's business, the less time you will have to think about how single you are. Besides, there are people out there who need you and what you offer to the kingdom. How selfish it is for us to deny them our gifts because we are so consumed with the desire to be married! That precious period is an opportunity to work toward accomplishing your goals and dreams. Here's an example of what I mean.

In 2006, I made a decision to pursue a business opportunity with a financial services company. I felt lead to start a business, and this was one that I truly believed in, so I went for it in the hopes that I would soon be able to quit my job and live in financial freedom for the rest of my life. Well, it didn't take long for me to realize that while it was definitely

You're not complete in a husband; you're not complete in a job; you're not even complete in yourself. Remember, always remember, that you are only ever complete in Christ Jesus.

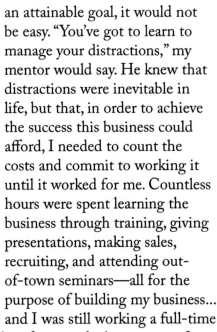

an attainable goal, it would not be easy. "You've got to learn to manage your distractions," my mentor would say. He knew that distractions were inevitable in life, but that, in order to achieve the success this business could afford, I needed to count the costs and commit to working it until it worked for me. Countless hours were spent learning the business through training, giving presentations, making sales, recruiting, and attending out-of-town seminars—all for the purpose of building my business... and I was still working a full-time job. The freedom I had to do all of that then far exceeds the amount of time I have now that I'm married and have someone else's time and needs to consider. As a single woman, my time was my own and my opportunity to explore what was important to me. It was the prime time for me to devote my time, energy, and resources to something other than myself or my partner. Remember, once you are married, all of those things are no longer yours. They are shared with another human being who has a mind and will of their own. Your interests are divided and your responsibility is to another person. Paul states this plainly in 1 Corinthians 7:32-34 (KJV) when he makes a claim in favor of the single lifestyle:

But I would have you without carefulness. He that is unmarried careth for the things that belong to the Lord: But he that is married careth for the things that are of the world, how he may please his wife. There is difference also between a wife and a virgin. The unmarried woman careth for the things of the Lord, that she may be holy both in body and in spirit: but she that is married careth for the things of the world, how she may please her husband.

Don't get me wrong, there are plenty of married folk out there accomplishing goals and dreams, but you cannot deny that it takes lots more sacrifice. So, *carpe diem!* While you are single, seize your moment and make the most of it.

Here is another way to make the most of your single state: use this time to become the type of person you'd like to marry. Every woman wants a good man, but "good" may mean different things to different people. To one woman, "good" may mean that he has a job with good pay and benefits, and that he doesn't mind sharing it. To another, it may mean that their man takes pride in his appearance and has a wonderful personality to match. To yet another, "good" may mean that their partner holds religious convictions and actually follows them in his daily life. Or it could mean that he's a combination of all of these things. Either way, whatever traits you desire in your mate, you should also possess. It's unfair to impose certain requirements on someone else that you are not willing to fulfill yourself. Do you have a good job with good pay and benefits and don't mind sharing? Do you take pride in your appearance and have a wonderful personality to match? Do you hold religious convictions and actually follow them in your daily life? Are you a good woman? I believe that you attract what you are, so do not be what you do not want.

Once I heard a woman say that before she lost fifty pounds, she thought people stayed away from her because she was fat. After she lost the weight, a friend told her that when she was fat, no one could stand her attitude. The revelation is it's not your physical state that repels people in most cases, it's what emanates from inside and how you make people feel when they are around you. Do you want a man who's confident? Then boost your own confidence. Do you want a man who has goals and the tenacity to accomplish them? Then be a go-getter yourself. Do you want a man who trusts you? Then learn to trust others. Do you want a man with high moral standards? Then raise yours. This idea is right in line with the principle of reaping and sowing found in Galatians 6:7 (KJV), which says, "Be not deceived; God is not mocked: for whatsoever a man soweth, that shall he also reap."

Anyone who has ever planted a seed knows that it takes time and consistent watering for that seed to grow, as does the seed of time we spend on self-improvement. No one accomplishes these things overnight, but consistent effort applied will produce a better you. So use what time you have as a single woman to figure out what exactly you need to improve, and then devote time to making the necessary changes in that area. Finally, give yourself the time to enjoy the fruit of your labor. If you adopt this mindset, you will surely reap a mate that has undergone some self-improvement of his own.

So, refuse to be like Cain whose problem was his vision, or the way he perceived the situation before him. What does that have to do with being single? EVERYTHING! Seeing singleness as rejection rather than as an opportunity is a trap that no one should be in. Instead, keep things in the right perspective. There was a time when I saw being single as being overlooked. Not many guys came my way, and I thought that was a bad thing. I thought it said something negative about me, but now I see that it was God keeping me hidden for THE ONE. He didn't want me to be exposed to a ton of dating experiences because he knew two things: first, He knew I couldn't handle the emotional rollercoaster of so many relationships; and second, He was keeping me for the prince he had for me.

So praise God for the opportunity and freedom to accomplish your goals and dreams, and praise Him for the opportunity to have time alone with Him. Staying busy keeps your mind in a good place, but rest assured: if you give God your best, He will give you His best in return.

The Waiting Room

1. In what ways can you increase your level of service to your ministry or to your community while you are still single?

    _____

    _____

2. What personal goals do you have on hold?

    _____

    _____

3. What is the first step in reaching that goal?

    _____

    _____

4. Now that you know you should get and stay busy, what might hinder you from accomplishing your goal?

    _____

    _____

 Say this confession in faith...

God has someone specifically designed just for me, and He is preparing us for each other. My single years are not a waste of time. God is using me exclusively for His divine purposes and rewarding me accordingly. This is my opportunity to pursue God and my purpose without distraction. I will make the most of each day that the Lord has blessed me with to live for Him and to enjoy His many blessings. This is the day that the Lord has made; I will rejoice and be glad in it (Psalms 118:24). At this very important time in my life, I give God my best and I expect His best in return. I put my hands to the plow of service and I won't look back, for God has a special work for me to do. I am steadfast, unmovable, and always abounding in the work of the Lord (1 Corinthians 15:58). Even as Boaz found Ruth while she was gleaning in the fields, my husband will find me being busy about my Father's business. I serve Him joyfully, and I will spend the balance of my singleness in pleasure. In Jesus's name.

Reflections—what does it all mean to you?

_____

_____

_____

_____

_____

_____

_____

CHAPTER 8

Offer Praise to God Continually

"In everything give thanks for this is the will of God concerning you." (1 Thessalonians 5:18 KJV)

Smile, woman of God, because you've got so much to be thankful for! Thank Him for everything, including your current marital status. God's timing is perfect, and He makes no mistakes. And your thankfulness now will prove that you're more devoted to the Bless*er* (God) and not the bless*ing* of a mate. After all, why would God give you something, knowing that it would take your attention completely off of Him? Let's be honest—you would feel the same way if a loved one preferred a gift you gave them over their relationship with you. God, as jealous as He is over you, is no different.

Again, you've got so many reasons to praise God. Just think about it! Oftentimes, the enemy leads us to focus on what we don't have, which makes us forget what we do have. Count your blessings, not your bumbles and relationship fumbles. Count your blessings, not just when things are good, but all the time. When you develop a consistent praise life and count your blessings, you will realize that you're walking in victory.

There is a gospel song titled "Praise is My Weapon," and when you think about it, that's so true. The Bible tells us that "The weapons of our warfare are not carnal, but mighty through God to the pulling down of strongholds" (2 Corinthians 10:4 KJV), meaning that our weapons are spiritual. It's when we resort to physical warfare that we lose the battle to Satan. How can you tell when you've lost? You lose your joy. You think only negative things about yourself and your situation. You begin to see the relationship glass half empty instead of half full. And worst of all, you lose your praise.

I began to fall into this rut about six months before I actually married my husband. We had been dating for a year, and I felt like we were on track to be married really soon. But when the conversation of plans for the future came up, I found out that the man I wanted to marry didn't have any to talk about, mainly because of a lack of finances. He hadn't had any concrete plans for us, at least not at the length that I expected him to have at this point in our relationship. He didn't know it at the time, but I had been saving up for our special day. I was so angry at him for not being where I was mentally or financially. I was frustrated with myself for wanting it so badly. But while it was an epic disappointment for me, it was also an eye-opener. Through that moment, God taught me that I had been so consumed with the idea of marriage that I was beginning to get out of my place of praise and my place of peace. Instead of continuing to trust Him, I began to worry about when I would get married.

When you develop a consistent praise life and count your blessings, you will realize that you're walking in victory.

My pastor always taught that one way to demonstrate trust in God is by sowing a seed, so one Sunday morning, I put my money where my mouth was and let the Holy Spirit lead me to sow the money I had begun to save for my wedding, and I sowed it with a praise. It was my way of putting my flesh under control and also my way of letting the devil and God both know that I trusted Him to give me the desires of my heart. I had never given that amount of money at one time in my entire life, but God honored my trust in Him. Six months later, Russell and I had the wedding of our dreams, honeymoon included, and we didn't even know where the money came from to pay for it all. God provided for me when I exercised my faith in Him, and it was my faith that allowed me to praise

God in spite of the obstacle I saw in front of me. *That* is engaging in true spiritual warfare!

Spiritual warfare requires putting on the whole armor of God that we learn about in Ephesians 6:11 and lifting up praise to God that confounds your enemy. "What are you doing praising when you don't have a man?" What am I doing NOT praising when I don't have a man? I've got more than enough reasons to praise God! I'm alive, I'm well, I've got food on my table, money in my pocket, shoes on my feet, a job, peace of mind, a car to drive, a good name, I'm saved, a child of God, and the list goes on and on and on. Even if you don't have all of the things I've named, you probably have a lot more that I didn't. Keeping praise in your mouth gets you that much closer to seeing your desires manifested.

Bottom line: if you do more complaining than praising, then you're not in God's will. Praise is optimism. Complaining is pessimism. Nobody wants to be around a constant complainer, not even your future husband. So, get a praise on your lips!

The Waiting Room

1. Name at least ten things you're thankful for.

   _____

   _____

2. How can you incorporate praise to God in your daily routine? Jot down your plan.

   _____

   _____

 ## *Say this confession in faith...*

I am a praiser and a worshipper, and I have so many things to praise God for. I give God praise in everything, even in my single state, for this is His will concerning me. I am content in my current situation because God has given me contentment. I am complete in Christ, nothing missing and nothing broken. I praise God for peace and favor. I praise Him for a sound mind, divine health, and strength. I praise Him for life more abundantly. I praise Him for my daily challenges because He makes me better through them. I praise Him for I am fearfully and wonderfully made. And I won't stop praising because I was created to worship and praise my God. I am a royal priesthood, a holy nation, a peculiar person to show forth the praises of Him who called me out of darkness into His marvelous light (1 Peter 2:9). Praise is comely for me (Psalms

33:1). It is my weapon of mass destruction to the forces of darkness at work in the atmosphere. No weapon formed against me shall prosper for I am covered by the blood of the Lamb (Isaiah 54:17). I am victorious and I win over the spirits of loneliness, insecurity, and inadequacy. They have no place in me at all because I know who I am in Christ. I am a beloved child of the Most High God and He loves and cherishes me. I am elect and precious, somebody special to God. I am called of God and chosen for such a time as this to represent His kingdom on the earth. I love and appreciate God for all He has done for me, and the proof of my gratitude toward Him and my trust in His goodness is my praise. In Jesus's name.

Reflections—what does it all mean to you?

_____

_____

_____

_____

_____

_____

_____

CHAPTER 9

Devote Time to Deep Conversation

"It is the glory of God to conceal a thing; but the honour of kings is to search out a matter." (Proverbs 25:2 KJV)

Once you've found someone who is worthy of time spent dating, ask questions—lots of them. Even the hard ones. No question is a dumb one to ask, unless, of course, the question does nothing to help you really get to know the person sitting across the table from you. Find out what his likes and dislikes are, his goals and dreams, his spiritual convictions...and then pay close attention. Time will tell if what he says lines up with what he does. If they don't, then you can make a more informed decision about whether or not any more time needs to be invested in the relationship.

My husband always jokes with me that I was talking marriage on the first date. He's exaggerating, but way in the back of my brain, I had an end in mind. Beginning with the end in mind helped me to be more intentional in my dating experience. I had just finished reading Steve Harvey's book *Act Like a Lady, Think Like a Man*, so I had my questions ready. "What are your goals? Where do you see yourself in five years? Ten years?" I spouted off each question and listened intently to the answers. I could see where I fit based on the assessment. Russell was cool on the outside, but on the inside, he was sweating bullets. He probably thought I was crazy, but he was not going to think I was gullible. Were all of his answers perfect and well thought out? No, but at least I knew from jump street what I was working with rather than being surprised later. Not all of my answers were stellar either, but at least the precedent was set.

Wait On God

What Every Single Woman Should Know to Receive God's Best!

I know that when we begin to really fall for someone, all we really want to do is spend time hugging up, watching movies, and going to dinner. We want them to whisper sweet nothings into our ears. But when you think about it, those sweet nothings really do mean just that—nothing—because they don't reveal the true character of the person you're with. Don't tell me something you think I want to hear, tell me something about yourself! That will really help me get to know you.

That's the purpose of dating, anyway. It's a long interview, and no question is off limits. Ask everything you want to know before you get married. Be ready to hear the answer and be ready to answer the questions yourself. Ask about his creditworthiness, his past relationships, his health, his desire or not for children. And then really listen to what the man has to say. Don't just listen with your ears. Listen with your eyes, too, and watch what he does. Notice patterns. Believe what his words and his actions together tell you. Pay attention to every red flag and challenge them because you'd rather challenge them now than later. And ladies, please don't assume that you can change him, because you can't. That's God's job. Take any concerns to God in prayer and He will show you how to proceed or how to retreat.

There are countless examples in the Bible of people seeking God for instructions on a matter and receiving them. The best example that I can think of is Jesus' instructions to the disciples when he sent them to preach the gospel to the lost sheep of Israel in Matthew 10:5-16. Not only did He tell them who to go see, he also told them where *not* to go—"...go not into the way of the Gentiles..." (Matthew 10:5 KJV, emphasis added). He told them what to say—"And as you go, preach, saying, 'The kingdom of heaven is at hand'" (Matthew 10:7

> **Being someone's wife is a very important assignment also, and it requires just as much instruction from God to be done correctly.**

KJV). He told them what to do when they got there—"Heal the sick, cleanse the lepers, raise the dead, cast out devils…" (Matthew 10:8 KJV). He even went so far as to tell them what they should not take and how they should not dress—"Provide neither gold, nor silver, nor brass in your purses, nor scrip for your journey, neither two coats, neither shoes nor yet staves…" (Matthew 10:9-10 KJV). Those are very detailed instructions for a very important assignment. Being someone's wife is a very important assignment also, and it requires just as much instruction from God to be done correctly. Jesus goes on to tell them that when they enter a city, that there would be those who are considered worthy of their presence and those who are not. It is with the worthy ones that they should fellowship.

> *"And into whatsoever city or town ye shall enter, enquire who in it is worthy; and there abide till ye go thence. And when ye come into the house, salute it. And if the house be worthy, let your peace come upon it: but if it be not worthy, let your peace return to you. And whosoever shall not receive you, nor hear your words, when ye depart out of that house or city, shake off the dust of your feet."*
> *(Matthew 10:11-14 KJV)*

Jesus' instructions are relevant to your dating experiences also. Your conversations with one another should help determine whether or not this man is worthy of your time and affection. If he is deemed worthy, then it is acceptable to bless him with your presence. If not, then walk away, leaving everything behind, and don't look back. Besides, if he's not someone you can see yourself marrying, then he shouldn't be someone you can see yourself dating, either.

To a Christian, the end game of any dating relationship should be marriage. If we're not working towards that, then what are we working towards? Are we just killing time? With our lives being like a vapor, you don't have that kind of time to waste. Besides, you're worth more and deserve more than that. So, should God instruct you to walk away from a dead-end relationship, don't worry. He even tells you how to avoid a bad breakup—"...be ye therefore wise as serpents, and harmless as doves" (Matthew 10:16 KJV). Utilizing the wisdom God provides in your prayer time with Him will help you to part ways without any major damage and still display His love in the process.

On the other hand, if God brings a man into your life that He has given the stamp of approval on and counts worthy of you, shout "Hallelujah!" You, my sister, are on the way to receiving the best man that God has to offer for you. I am a living witness that God's best is well worth the wait!

The Waiting Room

1. Write down three important questions to ask a potential husband.

   _____

   _____

   _____

2. What are your answers to those same questions?

   _____

   _____

   _____

   _____

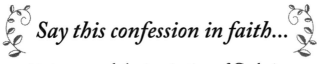

Say this confession in faith...

There is a spirit in me, and the inspiration of God gives me understanding. The Holy Spirit within me teaches me all things that He's received of God, so nothing catches me by surprise. He is my comforter and my guide into all truth. I seek the Word of God for counsel and wisdom in every matter. I expect to win in life and love, so I do not fight or carry out my daily affairs as one beating the air or with no purpose, but every conversation that I engage in and every encounter with those of the opposite sex has a purpose. I am spiritually sober, and the fruit of temperance is in full operation in my life. I am not deceived by charm, and flattering words do not move me. I am only moved by the Word of God. I am anxious for nothing, but in everything with prayer and supplication, I make my requests known unto God, and the peace of God which passes all understanding keeps my heart and mind through Christ Jesus (Philippians 4:6). In Jesus's name.

Reflections—what does it all mean to you?

_____

_____

_____

_____

_____

_____

About the Author

Briana G. Whitaker is the chairperson of the Young Women in Action Ministry (YWA) at Enon Missionary Baptist Church in Sumter, South Carolina, under the leadership of Pastor Stanley E. Hayes, Sr. and Elect Lady Julie Ann Hayes. For the past ten years, Briana has led the YWA ministry, a ministry with the purpose to win and prepare young women of God for kingdom service. At Enon, she also serves as a trustee, a church schoolteacher, a member of the choir, worship team, Arrows (youth) ministry, and Outreach. She was recently appointed as the vice-president of the Young Women's Auxiliary of the Sumter Baptist Missionary and Education Association, which serves twenty-one churches.

In 2005, she entered the education field, teaching middle school English language arts for seven years before becoming a school counselor. She holds a Master's degree in Education (Guidance and Counseling) from South Carolina State University in Orangeburg, South Carolina and a Bachelor's degree in English from the University of South Carolina in Columbia, South Carolina.

Briana is a former U.S. Army reservist and served her country in Operation Iraqi Freedom from March 2003 to March 2004. During her eight-year tenure in the military, she served as a print journalist with the 319th Mobile Public Affairs Detachment.

She enjoys writing and encouraging people, especially women, to seek God's best for their lives by giving Him their best. As a writer, she shares her personal experiences and insights in hopes that they will inspire others. Her blog provides soulful and insightful commentary on relationships and other various topics that are designed to provoke others to love and good works (Hebrews 10:24).

She currently resides in Sumter, South Carolina with her husband Russell. When she is not writing, she enjoys working out, singing, watching movies, and spending time with her family. Briana's mission is to be a positive example to the young women and girls within her ministry and in her daily life by practicing godly character and virtue.

You may visit her writing website at http://www.BrianaGWhitaker.com and her Facebook author page at www.facebook.com/BrianaGWhitaker. E-mail her at info@BrianaGWhitaker.com.